PARIPASSU

Poems
of Carolyn
& Us

Jay Harden

Azalea Art Press
Sonoma | California

© Jay Harden, 2023.
All Rights Reserved.

ISBN: 978-1-943471-70-6
Second Edition

Cover Art:
Sue Rolston Blackburn
September 1987

CONTENTS

Preface by Jay Harden   *i*

Eternally Young	1
Bloomed	3
The Holder of Wonder	4
Wherever She Was	5
Her Name Was	6
My Adored Shoulders	7
A Feast of Feeling	8
Not Enough	9
Sooner	10
For No Reason	11
Simple Adventures	12
One Night	13
Will I Be	14
A Time When	16
How Great is Memory	17
Simply Beautiful	18
Tall Trees	20
I Remember You	21
The Time	23
Paripassu	24
Carolyn	25
So Sane	26
Night is for Lovers	28
Blown Away	29

Room and Reason	32
The Turn	34
Always, Ahh	35
My Children	36
Eighteen After	38
Our Eight-Word Life	41
The Ever-Borning World	42
A Mere Yesterday	44
As I Age	45
Beyond the Visible	46
My Victory	47
Her and Heaven	48
Separate Roads	49
My Doubted Heaven	50
Always	51
I Never Will	52
About Carolyn Harden	***54***
About the Author	***57***
Book Orders	***58***
Contact	***58***

PREFACE

In Latin, *pari* means equal; *passu* means equal step. Here I combine them into one word, *paripassu*, to mean walking together, side-by- side, hand-in-hand.

That is the way Carolyn and I lived.

Carolyn and I exchanged about 300 letters and audio tapes during the time I was flying combat over Vietnam. Her voice had the serene lilt and infectious enthusiasm of a happy Southern Belle.

In 1990, a few years after she died, I wrote my first verses, now numbering over thirteen hundred. They were written in many places across this country, Europe, and South Asia.

I still write poems about love, war, life and death, spirituality, and some music lyrics. I keep a notepad by my bed and often wake in the night to jot a few lines. Most are a spring cleaning of my mind, inconsequential. The next morning, I am sometimes pleased at what I wrote and pursue it to fruition.

Here are some that I wrote about Carolyn.

Carolyn Harden

PARIPASSU

Carolyn & Jay Harden

Eternally Young

I knew you when you were thirteen.

You woke me with sweet,
    honest wiles
    and endless smiles.

You were eternally young.

I knew you when you were sixteen,
    my beauty with baton
    and brown hair shoulder down.

You were eternally young.

I knew you when you were a teacher,
    weaving your hands to wide-open eyes
    from one coast to another
    and in between.

You were eternally young.

I knew you when our children came;
    they were more like you,
    and you more like them.

You were eternally young.

I knew you when your loving grew bolder
    and you reached your wings
    to greater giving ways.

You were eternally young.

And I knew you when you were forty-two,
    braver than hope,

never so loved;
to me,
never so close,
when you were forty-two,
when you became eternally young.

Bloomed

As a boy he learned from his father
        to never bring his joy home.

That is,
        until he met her,
        and his heart flew open.

Then and there,
        their life bloomed.

The Holder of Wonder

Who among us
        is the holder of wonder?

Who keeps their sense of amazement?

Who marvels at the rain
        and welcomes the thunder?

And who tastes the wind?

And seasons each song?

And adores the creatures?

You do:
        living beyond mere body,
        singing your spirit,
        sharing all the worlds you know
        and those you seek
        with yourself and yours,
        creating things new
        all the while,
        going on
        and growing on
        pure as song.

Wherever She Was

A glance seeking,
      her hand reaching.

What could the world do
      but nod and smile?

That was our life
      over and again.

Days of gratitude burned by,
      fed from a fuse of care
      and laughing.

Autumns in Georgia;
      summer's sun in California;
      frost in New England;
      spring again in between.

I would live that way again.

There was magic
      wherever she was.

Her Name Was

They lived in the old days,
    the old days when
    everything was sweet.

The air was sweet,
    the grass under your toes,
    the running water,
    the light-footed animals,
    everything was sweet.

And the sweetest of all
    was her,
    the way she moved and touched,
    the way she gazed,
    and the softness of her breath
    and such honest words.

Life itself,
    all of it,
    was sweetest
    when she was around.

I never felt more innocent then,
    more at peace,
    or more loved.

And her name was mine.

My Adored Shoulders

When I smell *White Shoulders* now,
    I remember hers,
    more warm than white,
    more soft than fine, dusty powder.

And I am transported
    as gently as a dandelion seed
    across that wonderful meadow
    of our made memories.

There I am, head against her neck,
    cranked up on her bed beside her,
    the nurses closing the door after hours.

So happy to feel me falling asleep,
    she at last relaxes
    through her pain
    of approaching end,
    knowing I am safe
    against her body,
    so she can feel safe, too.

A Feast of Feeling

I move like water
>and leave with the wind
>and love more deeply
>approaching the end.

What is life
>but a feast of feeling
>floating in clouds,
>Heaven's own ceiling?

So much better this is
>than kneeling.

Now life is calling
>and I must go:
>our boat is ready
>for me to row.

Take you I will
>to drink your fill
>across the waters
>high up the hill.

There we will stand
>and constant stay,
>and shout our love
>to greet each day.

Not Enough

"Were you happy?" I asked her.

"Tell me the truth—like you always have."

And she said, "Yes."

Then,
       only then,
       I knew that was not enough,
       not enough
         for her to be gone.

Sooner

Death took you sooner,
       before Spring fully bloomed.

I and the world
       am left
       with a garden of weeds
       woven with thorns.

For No Reason

It broke me then.

In two.

Pieces.

And our children suffered.

A death for no reason
      can do that,
      when two loved
      as we did.

None will know
      all we created,
      or how happy
      we lived.

Simple Adventures

How wisely the way you left me,
    out of sight and not holding on,
    surrounded by people who loved you,
    with memories to rival the dawn.

Though I wish you had stayed with us longer,
    I completely trusted your soul
    much better than my strong longing.

We seem ageless as I grow old.

They all know you,
    our lovely descendants,
    and laugh the same way you would.

In their faces and hearts,
    I still see you,
    doing more than we ever could.

I can wait for our certain reunion
    in a place out of time unafraid
    to continue our simple adventures
    and build on the loving we made.

One Night

Love just disappeared one night in peace
    and everlasting sadness
    when life left with questions
    and a quiet shift of colors came,
    no longer real.

All I knew disappeared:
    loss wrapping everything and me
    in language I could not
    understand or express.

The hero of a thousand dreams came
    because I called,
    so love's yearning
    would one day
    again run true.

This day,
    this instant,
    holds every tomorrow
    I ever wanted.

I see your spirit again,
    and now I can
    show mine.

Will I Be

Will I still be lonely in heaven?

Who will smile at the end?

Is there really better,
        and will I meet her again?

Will I still be lonely in heaven?

A long time has passed since we parted.

The music was happier then.

That day I remember still comes each November.

We even had what might have been.

I have grown older,
        less bolder.

The zest is sometimes pretend.

The kids are now grown with lives of their own,
        unknown reflections of our best directions,
        and I am still missing my friend.

Will I be lonely in heaven?

The answer now I cannot know.

But I,
        in the meantime,
        continue with small rhymes
        and notice what wonders may flow.

Carolyn & Jay Harden

A Time When

Sometimes
    I still ache for you.

Not just your sparkle,
    beautiful enough,
    but for your glow,
    your always open arms
    disguised as your heart,
    for those times
    when I feel it necessary
    to taste the food of your love.

I know I will never
    have it again,
    but still,
    I steal some magical hope
    for that time
    when we thought less,
    and cared more,
    and lived lightly
    in the moments
    of each other.

How Great Is Memory

You're reading your book in my chair.

How peaceful that seems.

You glance up and smile and my loneliness lifts away:
    you content with us.

With a look,
    a smile,
    a move,
    your beauty reaches in
    and bounces out mine.

Again,
    we make our calm connection,
    defeating a busy world.

We create presence,
    so love leaps up again.

How great is memory,
    my memory of you.

Simply Beautiful

She was beautiful.

She really was.

Then she said:
    "You are beautiful."

And she believed it.

I could see it in the way
    she revealed her smile
    and relaxed her eyes.

And I believed she believed it.

I knew she did.

So,
    I settled for believing she believed,
    for I had trouble believing;
    I had such trouble.

Her belief was enough back then;
    I could see no beauty in me.

I could feel the remnants of my ruins,
    the beaten structures,
    but all I could worthy see
    in me
    was through her.

Then my love conspired
    against my battered me.

She assaulted my disbelieving lie
    and shared her belief
    in my beauty:
    confirming her truth,

      which was not mine,
      with another—me.

Now I doubted myself,
      doubting my clear ugliness,
      once comfortable,
      because I trusted her
      and her truth
      more than my own.

My discomfort became so intolerable
      that I had to fight
      the long-delayed struggle
      for my fragile life
      and very soul.

My darkest ego and my innocent child
      made high combat
      on the loneliest plains of existence:
      one to live
      and the other to die.

To one side,
      she stood,
      a beacon of beauty,
      with unassailable faith
      in my own great goodness:
      my inspiration to slaughter ego
      with love and a sword of light.

On my field of victory,
      I danced myself
      into the present,
      knowing I was
      beautiful.

Tall Trees

She would look into my eyes softly,
        stroke my fingers
        with such ease,
        and say:
        "It will be fine;
        you will be fine;
        you *are* fine."

Then with a sure small smile,
        I knew the moment was great
        and the future mattered less.

You and I are tall trees,
        wonderfully growing.

Feel that,
        feel only that.

I Remember You

You are still
      so real to me.

I read your letters
      to me in Vietnam
      for the second time
      after 40 years,
      and you come back
      into my life.

Your soothing lilt
      captures my ears,
      then a remembered smile,
      your familiar breeze,
      and this old heart
      creaks open
      a little more.

I remember you
      that young,
      that certain,
      that resilient,
      that alive;
      how we teamed up
      toward an unknown world.

What I would give now
      to whisper in your ear
      and cause that laughter.

Surely something so wonderful
      as we had
          cannot have been imagined,
          cannot have left the stage.

Perhaps your teaching
        did awaken other hearts
        like mine,
        and prove love given
        is never lost
        and always
        worth the loss.

The Time

The time you warmed my face with your hands,
    the time you saw through my sighs,
    the time you stole my secret pain with a kiss,
    the time you felt my awkward reach
    that yielded our children.

The time you laughed
    and made my hope fresh again.

The time you relaxed,
    so I relaxed, too.

The time you showed the way
    we went through,
    the time you gave away
    precious time,
    the time you spent building me
    so I could build you,
    the time you loved
    and never stopped,
    the time…the time…the time.

Paripassu

I open my shirt
        and sing to you
        my best song again,
        but you cannot hear,
        like letters I write
        on water.

Spring has gone with you,
        leaving only your laugh,
        still repeating
        in my uncensored heart,
        like the rain of your kisses
        in my head.

We once knocked
        the world to attention
        and children bloomed.

This is what I remember
        when young,
        so fearless.

I learned to believe
        in life after death
        because we gave each other
        life before death,
        paripassu:
        the gratitude of being together
        by another name,
        without time.

Carolyn

So easy it was
> to be at ease with her:
> a face matching
> the morning sky,
> fresh and open,
> promising a safe mystery.

I took the time,
> and she decloaked my heart,
> before any chance
> to surrender.

Perhaps that playful voice;
> perhaps that safe smile:
> really, it was her eyes
> where my love finally rested,
> that honestly revealed:
> you matter and I understand.

She was the loveliest
> possibility I ever saw
> walk through the sunlight of Athens.

Hers was a shorter season,
> but every day with her
> was its own eternity.

So Sane

Those crazy fluttering flowers,
      bouncing over breezes,
      floating on the wind swells,
      tickling my attention,
      bending wings into a smile,
      waving at me,
      like the little girl
      she was and stayed,
      forever.

This is how I remember her,
      constant and welcoming,
      she who loved my soul.

If ever there was a synonym for butterfly,
      it was her name,
      Carolyn,
      a sound that rolled out of me
      like a warm buttered roll rolls in,
      effortless and natural,
      made for my body;
      she fed my hunger.

This woman who nurtured me,
      and them,
      as easy as real love allows,
      more comforting than
      the things she left:
      her prisms,
      her sliced shells,
      the daisies,
      and those yellow butterflies
      she adored
      and now inhabits.

Sure, I was crazy—about her—
    a crazy I wish on all of you,
    a crazy beyond reasonable men,
    a deep and daring crazy,
    like sticking your head out the window
    trying to fly,
    the kind of crazy
    that makes parents speechless,
    before admiration,
    that makes others wish more
    and regret less.

You see, she and I were
    crazy beautiful together,
    like her yellow flying flutterer that visits.

In our short partner time,
    never did I feel so happy,
    so peaceful,
    or so sane.

Night Is for Lovers

Night is for lovers.

We sit in the dark
        and talk endlessly,
        connecting in one breath,
        laughing inexplicably,
        sharing secrets,
        discovering our way.

The darkness invites us
        to honesty others
        never understand.

Here is where we build our treasure house,
        our Place of Peace.

Here is where we find our hopes.

Here,
        beneath this mantle of stillness,
        we love,
        and the present stands still.

Blown Away

I am still blown away
      by your beauty
      and the sparks
      that leap
      from your soul.

It's been twenty years
      since you left me
      and my love
      remains constant,
      not cold.

By now
      I should have forgotten;
      I expect this is
      truer for you.

But your eyes take me back
      with each photo
      and I re-feel your warmth
      reaching through.

Why weren't you just ordinary:
      a fairly good wife,
      a nice friend?

Instead,
      you made children
      just like you,
      and loved me and them
      without end.

I try and I try to forget you,
      but I can't dismiss
      what we had.

You live in my pocket as always
        and smile at me
          when I get sad.

Could you please
        let me hold you
         just once more?

Hear your voice say
        how much
         you love me?

Then I think I can
        let you go freely
        and live the way
        you lived to me.

Carolyn Harden

Room and Reason

You gave me room and reason
> in our continued season
> to live with you and laugh,
> splash babies in the bath.

We held hands together,
> you talked about whatever.

I reveled in your glance
> and bloomed us past romance.

We started out like others,
> our fathers and our mothers,
> then strong we grew and grew
> so much beyond just two.

We found the joy in wonder,
> cuddled in the thunder,
> told our dreams aloud,
> and celebrated crowds.

You were always funny;
> I knew we needed money.

Yet with the gift we had
> we overcame the sad.

You energized the world,
> and from afar you knew
> what I admired in you.

To them you were my wife,
> to me the zest for life.

You finally made me see
> your real belief in me.

The four of us kept growing
        faster and more knowing,
        gaining age with grace,
        skipping place to place.

Our life grew richer more,
        with better love in store.

Then,
        family in full stride,
        you were called inside.

We lingered hand in hand
        remembering the band.

With "I love you" I know
        at last,
        you had to go.

This love that ran
        so deep
        explains why
        I still weep.

Yes, we keep on kissing
        and remember who is missing,
        for what we learned from you
        will always bloom anew.

We fill our separate seasons
        with enthusiastic reasons,
        for others need us now—
        we know, we show them how.

Our lives may rearrange,
        yet some things never change:
        yes, life is where we live
        and love is what we give!

The Turn

Oh, the joys of ordinary living,
      the "dailies" she called them,
      the noise and toys of our children,
      the sweet sweat of doing,
      the taste of every morning,
      that look as she turned her face to mine
      and smiled,
      all those little things that are everything.

What I miss is her kiss,
      her lilting laugh,
      the tilt of her head toward me,
      as if I were more important than her,
      as if I were a certain part of her joy,
      like she is mine still,
      the tender blown kisses
      and fair flash of her eyes
      that saw everything OK, as it is.

She was my reassuring comfort
      when the world overwhelmed
      and I bent with the whipping wind;
      she knew I would not break.

She endowed me with my own sense of wonder,
      like today when her yellow butterfly
      danced among my dandelions,
      then settled for a rest in one;
      I knew, simply knew,
      she had come to see how I am.

Then she left on that dandelion a promise
      to someday, somewhere,
      laugh with me again.

Always, Ahh

I have never known such love
    so simple
    and adorned with laughter.

You, who caused me to care so,
    left your warmth
    in every cell of mine.

Now I smile like you,
    an infection somehow passed on
    to our fresh, bubbling genes,
    the secret taught
    that I cannot explain.

They know your generous,
    caressing wonder.

And this is the sound
    it makes:
    ahh,
    always, ahh.

My Children

I pause and peer into the cause
      of my recorded life,
        then smile within the mistiness,
      remembering my wife,
      and children made together
      we sought to understand.

They blossomed free
      and gave to me
      completion as a man.

We learned more
      than we taught them,
      to feel more than before.

We gazed new ways
      into their days,
      a spacious magic store.

And from a distance hoping,
      our hearts turned strong
      with theirs.

In watching,
      we remembered and answered
      our own prayers.

We played a time together,
      foot racing with the sun.

She twinkled,
      sprinted into dusk,
      and joined the stars as one.

My children,
> I adore you
> for many priceless things,
> for granting me a kingdom
> and demonstrating wings.

Eighteen After

We weren't special,
    we were just magnificently human—
    and you missed it;
    you missed the children
    growing up
    and becoming real!

You missed the grandchildren
    who proved our experiment!

We were foolish enough,
    with stars in our eyes,
    to go for it all,
    to create together
    a new kind of family,
    one we had never seen,
    except in our spirit.

We dared and we won it all!

You should see the little one:
    just like you,
    the very best of you
    and none of the damage,
    a stunning example of possibility,
    just like her sister.

And the boy…
    he is fearless and beautiful
    and powerful and smart
    and,
    most of all,
    he is kind,
    too.

You should be here
        to see them bloom.

How I'd love to tell you…
        I could not in my imagination
        conceive of improvement.

You missed it all, you goofed up;
        you left too soon and
        now I am angry,
        for I have no one, not one,
        to share this great victory
        that is ours alone!

No one to tell the secret remembrances,
        no one to congratulate
        and say we really did it,
        we even surpassed our dream!

Through us,
        five more are gifts to the universe,
        so much in need of conscious beings.

I have no worries about them
        and wish I could tell you.

They will be protected all their lives
        by the gods and goddesses,
        the saints,
        the angels,
        the beings of light,
        the great spirit,
        the source of everything.

You see,
>	my darling,
>	they embody the hidden hope
>	of every mortal,
>	models for the future
>	when men and women
>	realize the truth of being
>	on this earth.

I am so sorry for you
>	and for myself
>	that you are not here
>	to see the splendor
>	that two through love
>	can make real.

I cannot be angry at you for long.

I just wish you were here
>	to celebrate with me our victory
>	of heart over mind,
>	of daring over restraint,
>	of love over fear.

When we meet again,
>	I will grasp you in my arms
>	once more,
>	and look into your eyes,
>	and say with all my passion,
>	I, your fellow conspirator,
>	thank you for us,
>	in defeating the illusion of history.

We went for it all and we *won*.

And what we discovered was,
>	more like us are possible.

Our Eight-Word Life

I winked.

She laughed.

We loved.

She died.

The Ever-Borning World

She is no longer at the table,
        and now I eat alone:
        her wit,
        a memory;
        her wisdom,
        my comforting companion.

How is it that beauty leaves
        and construction stays,
        another work in progress?

Heaven still hovers over me,
        twinkling and blessing.

Somehow,
        she has become part of me.

Somehow,
        I always knew this life
        did not escape by grace unaffected.

In my way,
        I carry on her hopes and mine,
        watching our children
        gather the glimpses they need
        and build more simple sanity
        to softly fuel the ever-borning world
        that brought us here
        and will take us together there.

Carolyn
at Disneyland, California
with the Rabbit from *Alice in Wonderland*
1966

A Mere Yesterday

I wonder if she knows
      how much I miss her.

That would comfort me.

So gentle,
      so soft,
      were those strokes to my soul,
      her presence spilling out
      a freshness to live.

She smiled like a child
      and laughed so easily
      that I learned in part
      my better heart
      being born every day,
      a little bit of delight
      helping our cozy home.

No one else will ever know
      that depth of her,
      our forgiveness of each other,
      every fine dream,
      or how vast my cherishing
      these words do hint.

So magnificent
      and glorious a time,
      a mere yesterday.

As I Age

If I look back into my memory of you,
    I see a handmade video of evenings
    wrapping us together,
    your gentle hand
    around my shoulder
    and glances of brown
    catching the moonlight,
    and a few words,
    not many,
    like yellow and gold leaves
    lazing down a creek
    sustaining our connection,
    as whispered exchanges do.

Those memories have children of their own now,
    each a fresh verse
    of the same song
    themed by life,
    fed by love,
    as I age.

Beyond the Visible

I have been a boy;
    I have been a son;
    I have been a husband;
    I have been a father,
    now a grandfather;
    and I have been me.

Sometimes I cry so simply
    for the unexpressed beauty within.

Privately alone with that truth,
    that difference I feel,
    that unique treasure of me
    I accept.

I submit to the wonder of that moment,
    not knowing its meaning.

How could she be so real,
    so lovely,
    so lovable,
    so loving,
    then so gone?

Because that is the arc of life.

Where did my love of love go?

Lost along the road;
    I'm no more lost than the next man.

Kindness is everywhere
    and I must find it again,
    beyond the surface of the visible
    where everything of value lies.

My Victory

I overcame your intolerable cancer
        and kept on living.

My victory outshines that loss.

Our children carry the best of you,
        and their children, too.

Their smiles are partly yours,
        their hearts at least as open.

They are my memory of you.

What we built grows in them,
        so you are never far.

Though I miss the tangible you,
        the taste of our happiness
        lingers on my lips.

The smile of our secrets
        warms my lonesome winters,
        and I feel you
        whenever butterflies need noticing
        and the wind and rain
        blow soft on me,
        smelling like new life.

Her and Heaven

More she slips
      quietly into my presence
      and Heaven holds
      my imagined hopes.

Is she lonely there
      as I am here,
      another wondering heart?

My waiting soul
      ponders that
      with a sigh.

Ah, I will rather choose
      to believe in
      endurable us.

Then, now,
      and always.

Separate Roads

I'll go down and so will you,
    down our separate roads.

I'll walk with you and you with me,
    down our separate roads.

Where you slip will be my hand,
    and if I fall,
    with me you stand,
    down our separate roads.

Our gains will help us bloom and find
    what we must learn and leave behind,
    down our separate roads.

Then when our paths combine anew,
    we look at all that we've been through,
    happier and wiser, too,
    and loving more what we will do
    each moment now,
    alone and joined,
    down our separate roads.

My Doubted Heaven

It haunts me
    night and day.

If I had been better,
    then would she stay?

If I had been kinder,
    angry less,
    she would have been blessed.

I stumbled at love,
    and tried too hard
    to be her everything,
    her rock,
    her savior,
    her graceful man,
    her best companion.

I failed to be
    what she deserved.

A part of me broke
    and died with her.

I ache to talk
    with Carolyn again
    in some gentle realm,
    some way.

Every day,
    I wander lonely
    for her gaze,
    her voice,
    her love,
    her touch,
    and her shining happiness
    in my doubted heaven.

Always

So many hints of wonder;
        cold wind down my collar.

All the birds are gone
        and she had left forever.

The wonder memories
        hurt heavy most.

I see her smile
        in every reflected light,
        bright as the stars
        on a clear night.

Too soon, too soon,
        so long ago,
        when I was handsome
        and she loved me:

Does she even now,
        as I her?

The mystery
        of her magic
        still enchants me.

I can see
        her fresh face
        on the wind,
        alive in swaying daisies,
        greeting me
        with hello bursts of life.

Never will I forget her;
        always will I love her:
        always, always, and always.

I Never Will

The past is never past,
      but a push to make the present last,
      a gentle mystery in my imagination,
      like the discovered dandelion
      in my freshly mowed lawn.

I am older now,
      gray and spotted,
      or could be
      in my memory.

Our love endures
      perhaps because
      we were so constant
      and equally lovable.

We valued our slice of time,
      and it ran fast,
      breathless and beautiful.

How do I thank her
      for being real then,
      for being real still?

Across the universe
      I still hold her in my arms.

I never said goodbye
      and I never will.

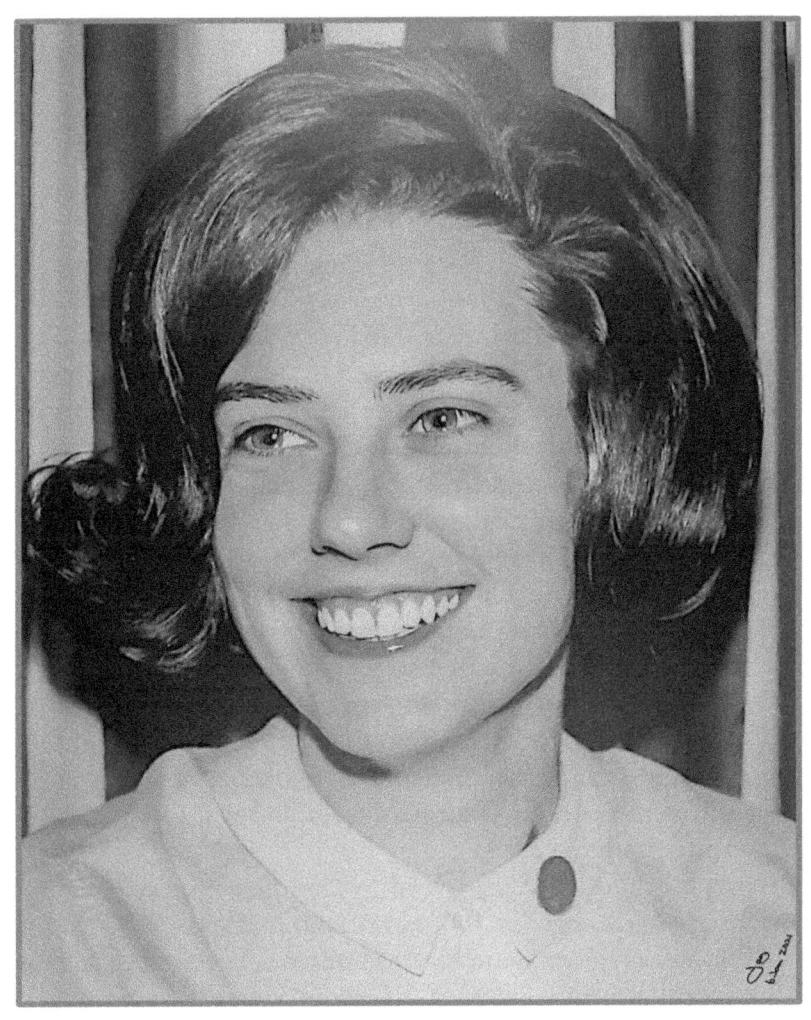

Carolyn Harden

ABOUT CAROLYN HARDEN

We met in the fall of 1958 when I was fifteen and she was fourteen. Less than a year later, on May 9, 1959, we planned to be married as soon as one of us graduated from college. This was our secret.

Carolyn was a student in my mother's high school algebra class. She was on the Athens High School girl's tennis team from 1961 to 1962, taught me how to play, and bought me my first racquet.

She was a born teacher; it was her heart's desire. Our high school principal told Carolyn she was not college material and should go to secretarial school, but I convinced her otherwise. She graduated from the University of Georgia in three years and was elected to three scholastic honorary societies. At Georgia, she was also a member of Alpha Chi Omega sorority and president of her pledge class.

The principal apparently did not remember her when he was on the County Board of Education and hired her as a first-grade teacher. She taught first grade at Childs Street Elementary School in Athens from 1965-1966 and wrote a groundbreaking paper on "Readiness" for the school in 1966. She taught kindergarten, first grade, and remedial reading at different times in Georgia, Massachusetts, California, and Missouri.

Carolyn was a lead teacher for Project Head Start in Georgia in 1966 and again in 1968-1969. She was an instructor and kindergarten teacher at the Child Development Center, of Florissant Valley Community College, St. Louis, from 1974-1975. She also supervised student teachers at Webster College, Webster Groves, Missouri in 1975 and taught at Meramec Community College, St. Louis, Missouri from 1984-1987. Carolyn also found time to be a Brownie Scout Troop Leader from 1976-1978.

From 1979-1987, she was a private educational consultant teaching classes on parenting, child growth, child development and self-esteem, and creative activities for children on over 200 separate occasions to over 4,000 people for 56 different clients.

She also developed special education programs for Kirkwood United Methodist Church Preschool, Parkway East Junior High School, and Ivy Chapel School for Young Children in St. Louis, Missouri. She developed and taught her *Parents as Teachers* classes to parents in the Kirkwood School District, St. Louis.

Had I to choose one word that described and embodied Carolyn and her life that affected our living together, it would have to be the Greek word *entheos* that means "one out of God." She was wholly and completely alive with *enthusiasm* all her life, one of her many qualities that charmed me into devotion.

Carolyn positively impacted the lives of innumerable children during her teaching career, and I was her witness. I quietly see the effect of her life on our daughter, son, and five grandchildren.

She was a gift to the world and the best thing that ever happened to me.

The photograph of Carolyn on page 51 is dated November, 1970. She was 26 years old.

Author Jay Harden
© *Journey Carolyn Collins*

ABOUT THE AUTHOR

Jay Harden grew up in Georgia envying the eagles and hawks, ditching his shoes in summer, and adventuring the alleys, trees, and creeks. Since the beginning, his life has been defined by moments of truth, planned and unplanned.

He survived air combat in Vietnam and navigated his B-52 crew safely home 63 times. After active duty he served in the Missouri Air National Guard and pursued a science career in the Department of Defense, retiring in 1997.

While at the DoD, he helped develop the world's first digital mapping system and co-authored a ground-breaking technical handbook on cartography that was widely distributed in the Defense Department and beyond. He has since published in numerous anthologies and privately published multiple volumes of family history, poetry, and journals.

He now spends his days writing, painting, photographing, playing guitar, and learning from his five amazing grandchildren.

For more copies of Paripassu
please visit:
Lulu.com, Amazon,
Barnes & Noble
and other online venues

To Contact the Author:
please email
Jay@JayHarden.com

To Contact the Publisher
please email:
Azalea.Art.Press@gmail.com

www.ingramcontent.com/pod-product-compliance
Lightning Source LLC
LaVergne TN
LVHW011430080426
835512LV00005B/363